DOLORES HUERTA

A HERO TO MIGRANT WORKERS

WITHDRAWN

BY
SARAH WARREN

ILLUSTRATED BY
ROBERT CASILLA

MARSHALL CAVENDISH CHILDREN

Marshall Cavendish Corporation, 99 White Plains Road, Tarrytown, NY 10591
www.marshallcavendish.us/kids

Library of Congress Cataloging-in-Publication Data
Warren, Sarah.
Delores Huerta : a hero to migrant workers / by Sarah Warren ;
illustrated by Robert Casilla. — 1st ed.
p. cm.
ISBN 978-0-7614-6107-4 (hardcover) — ISBN 978-0-7614-6108-1 (ebook)
1. Huerta, Dolores, 1930—Juvenile literature. 2. Women labor
leaders—United States—Biography—Juvenile literature. 3. Mexican American
women labor union members—Biography—Juvenile literature 4. Mexican
American migrant agricultural laborers—Labor
unions—Organizing—History—Juvenile literture. 5. Migrant agricultural
laborers—Labor unions—United States—History—Juvenile literature. I.
Casilla, Robert, ill. II. Title.
HD6509.H84W37 2012
331.4'7813092—dc22
[B]
2011016403

The illustrations are rendered in watercolor with pastels.
Book design by Anahid Hamparian
Editor: Marilyn Brigham

Printed in Malaysia (T)
First edition
10 9 8 7 6 5 4 3 2 1

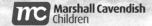

Marshall Cavendish
Children

To Susie, Ruth, Lillian, Jessy, Lisa, Deby, and of course, Dolores—
awesome moms, outstanding women

—S.W.

To Carmen Casilla, my wife and closest friend

—R.C.

THIS IS DOLORES.

Dolores is a teacher, but her students are too hungry to listen. They are too sick to play. They have no shoes to wear at recess.

Dolores is a detective.

She follows the kids home. She asks the moms why their kids are hungry and sick. She asks the dads why their children don't have shoes.

The parents say their bosses don't pay them enough money for good food or new clothes or a visit to the doctor. These parents work hard. They pick grapes all morning. They pick grapes all afternoon. They pick grapes until night, but they are paid too little and shoes cost too much.

Dolores is a friend.

The farm workers tell her their troubles. They don't get fresh water. They don't get bathroom breaks. Their hard work is worth more than what they are paid. Friends look out for each other, so Dolores decides to take a stand.

Dolores is a warrior.

She walks right up to the bosses. She asks them to give the workers rest breaks and to let them stay home when they're sick. She asks each boss to pay the workers enough money for shoes and books and medicine.

They say no. The bosses say that if they give the workers more money, they will have to raise the price of the grapes. Then nobody will buy them.

This excuse is not good enough. The kids still need food. The kids still need medicine. The kids still need shoes.

UNFAIR WORK CONDITIONS
UNFAIR TO WORKERS
STRIKE
STRIKE
HUELGA STRIKE
STRIKE HUELGA
TO

Dolores is an organizer.

She asks the people to strike. They will not work until the bosses start to listen. Instead of picking grapes, the workers stand outside the farms. They shout. They sing. They write STRIKE and YES, IT CAN BE DONE! on signs they hold up high.

Dolores is a storyteller.

When the bosses won't change their minds, she tells stories that show why their farms are not healthy places to work. She tells shoppers. She tells crowds. She tells television reporters. She tells senators, mayors, and governors. Many people listen. Some people don't.

Dolores is a peacemaker.

She doesn't use violence to make the bosses pay attention; she grabs them with her words. She encourages the workers to use their voices, too, until the bosses learn how to be fair.

Dolores is a mother.

Changing the bosses' minds takes a long time, and she misses her kids. The mothers and fathers on strike miss their kids, too. While some workers argue with the bosses, others watch the children play and keep them safe.

Dolores is a woman.

Some people think she should quiet down and let the men do the talking. Dolores just gets louder. She asks other women to speak up, too. Their voices rise up together, booming over the farm, roaring into the city, rumbling across the country.

Dolores is a fortune-teller.

She predicts the future. She tells the bosses that if they don't pay workers well for their hard work, the workers will stop picking the grapes, and the grapes will rot. She tells the bosses that if people hear workers are mistreated, nobody will buy their grapes.

All of Dolores's predictions start coming true. The farms become empty. The grapes are left on the vines. Nobody will pick them. Nobody will buy them.

Finally, the strikes begin to work. The bosses tell the workers that if they come back, they can take rest breaks. The bosses will raise their pay. The workers will get money to buy food, medicine, and shoes for their children. The workers are happy, but Dolores is not finished.

Dolores is a hunter.

She hunts for other bosses who need to take better care of their workers. Dolores tells them to listen . . . or else.

Dolores is a teacher.

She teaches people how to work as a team. She teaches people how to take care of each other.

This is Dolores.

TIMELINE

April 10, 1930 Dolores Fernández is born in New Mexico. It is the Great Depression. Americans don't have much money and jobs are few.

1933 Dolores's parents, Alicia and Juan, divorce.

1936 Alicia moves her family to Stockton, California. She runs a hotel and restaurant for migrant workers and lets them stay even if they cannot pay. Dolores becomes a Girl Scout. She plays piano, dances flamenco, marches in the band, and sings in the choir. She cans fruit to earn money. Some people do not treat Dolores fairly. A teacher thinks Mexican American students aren't smart enough to write well. Dolores is a talented writer, but the teacher believes Dolores must have turned in papers written by someone else.

1947 Dolores graduates from Stockton High School and attends the University of the Pacific.

1948 Dolores gets married and has two children. In time, the marriage ends.

1955 Dolores graduates from college and becomes a teacher. She sees that her students are too hungry to learn. These families need help. Dolores joins the Community Service Organization (CSO). She visits workers in their homes and on the farms. She registers workers to vote and introduces them to reading and writing classes. Dolores pushes for laws to protect Spanish-speaking Californians. She marries her second husband, Ventura Huerta.

1956 Dolores meets César Chávez, another volunteer. They both want farm workers to be treated fairly. Dolores travels to many farms. She depends on donations to provide for her family.

1961 Dolores and Ventura end their marriage.

1962 Dolores helps her friend César start the National Farm Workers Association (NFWA). César is the president. Dolores is the vice president.

Spring 1965 The NFWA helps underpaid rose farm workers organize a strike. In less than a week, the grower asks the workers to come back. He agrees to pay them higher wages.

Fall 1965 Dolores and César join another union in a strike against grape growers. The growers use farm equipment to cover the workers with dust. They spray them with bug poison, scare them with dogs, call them names, and beat them. They bring in new workers and ignore the workers on strike.

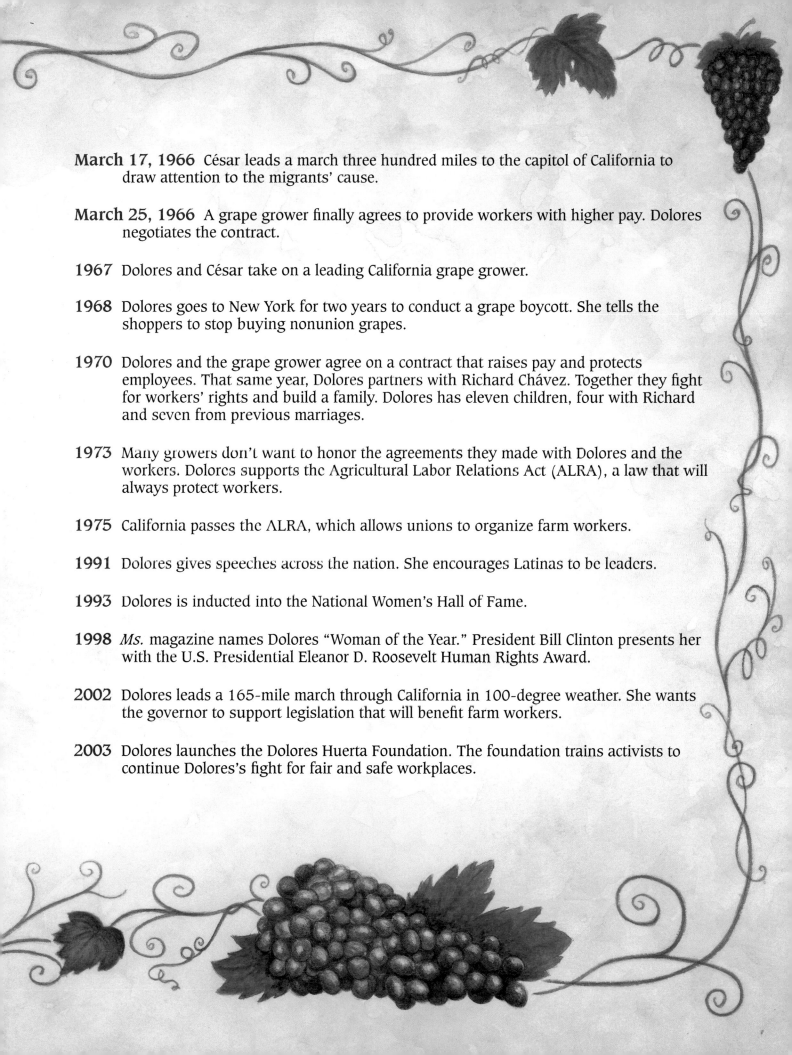

March 17, 1966 César leads a march three hundred miles to the capitol of California to draw attention to the migrants' cause.

March 25, 1966 A grape grower finally agrees to provide workers with higher pay. Dolores negotiates the contract.

1967 Dolores and César take on a leading California grape grower.

1968 Dolores goes to New York for two years to conduct a grape boycott. She tells the shoppers to stop buying nonunion grapes.

1970 Dolores and the grape grower agree on a contract that raises pay and protects employees. That same year, Dolores partners with Richard Chávez. Together they fight for workers' rights and build a family. Dolores has eleven children, four with Richard and seven from previous marriages.

1973 Many growers don't want to honor the agreements they made with Dolores and the workers. Dolores supports the Agricultural Labor Relations Act (ALRA), a law that will always protect workers.

1975 California passes the ALRA, which allows unions to organize farm workers.

1991 Dolores gives speeches across the nation. She encourages Latinas to be leaders.

1993 Dolores is inducted into the National Women's Hall of Fame.

1998 *Ms.* magazine names Dolores "Woman of the Year." President Bill Clinton presents her with the U.S. Presidential Eleanor D. Roosevelt Human Rights Award.

2002 Dolores leads a 165-mile march through California in 100-degree weather. She wants the governor to support legislation that will benefit farm workers.

2003 Dolores launches the Dolores Huerta Foundation. The foundation trains activists to continue Dolores's fight for fair and safe workplaces.

LEARN MORE ABOUT DOLORES HUERTA

Books

Doak, Robin S. *Dolores Huerta: Labor Leader and Civil Rights Activist*. Minneapolis: Compass Point Books, 2008.

Garcia, Mario T. (editor). *A Dolores Huerta Reader*. Albuquerque: University of New Mexico Press, 2008.

Garza, Hedda. *Latinas: Hispanic Women in the United States*. Albuquerque: University of New Mexico Press, 2001.

Gillis, Jennifer Blitzen. *American Lives: Dolores Huerta*. Chicago: Heinemann Library, 2005.

Miller, Debra A. *Dolores Huerta: Labor Leader*. Farmington Hills: Thomson Gale/Lucent Books, 2006.

Articles

Huerta, Dolores. "Being more than a good mother involves activism," McClatchey Tribune News Service, May 2, 2005, page 1.

Williams, Jasmin K. "Classroom extra—Women's History Month Edition—Fighting for 'La Causa'," *New York Post*, March 9, 2005, page 94.

Websites

The struggle for workers' rights continues. Visit www.ufw.org to learn more about the history and successes of the **United Farm Workers** (originally the NFWA).

The Dolores Huerta Foundation trains people to team up and battle inequality. Visit www.doloreshuerta.org to learn more about Dolores and her continued fight against prejudice and injustice.

Farmworker Justice educates and empowers migrant workers. It investigates and communicates how actions made by our government will influence the lives of workers. Learn more: www.farmworkerjustice.org

The **Honoring the Hands** project shows the impact of the migrant health movement on the lives of workers. www.honoringthehands.com

Teacher Resources

Teaching for Change gives students and educators the resources to work for justice. Learn more at: www.teachingforchange.org

This Is My Home provides educators with tools to nurture human rights in the classroom. Teachers can register for this Minnesota-based program at: www.hrusa.org/thisismyhome